I am putting this information at the beginning of this book because it is the most important of all. There are thousands of companies out there that are conning new authors into signing over their rights and royalties to them. And, even worse, they are charging the authors to do it. Even worse than that, many tens of thousands of authors have fallen for it. Don't be one of them.

There are only five big publishers in the United States that are legit. There are several smaller legit publishers that can traditionally sign an author as well. I am not listing them because this industry is constantly changing, and by this time next year, the names or companies may be different. I want this information to be as accurate as possible for years. An internet search can help distinguish a real publisher from a fake one. I'll go into how to spot a con publisher later in this book.

The person most likely to fall for a scam is the author who wants to be signed by a traditional publisher so badly they can just feel it. If you are an author and you think you will never make it unless you are signed, you are the most vulnerable. If you are dead set on being a traditionally published author, go at it the right way. Don't let your hunger and lack of knowledge of the publishing industry cloud your judgment.

There are some rules that a new author can follow to keep from getting conned by a crook or criminal. Do not let your craving for success cause you to make bad decisions that will drain your bank account and kill your dream of making a living as an author. Follow these very simple rules and you will be far less likely to be taken by a con publisher, agent, or marketing firm. Remember, if you sign with a fake, a real one likely will never touch you.

RULES TO LIVE BY AS AN AUTHOR:

1) **A real publisher DOES NOT solicit authors.** A real publisher is never going to solicit you in any way by social media, message, phone, or text message, at a convention, or anywhere else. If you are being solicited by someone calling themselves a publisher, run. It is a scam. There are no exceptions to this rule.

2. **A real agent DOES NOT solicit authors.** A real agent is never going to solicit you in any way by social media, message, phone, or text message, at a convention, or anywhere else. If you are being solicited by someone calling themselves an agent, run. It is a scam. There are no exceptions to this rule.

3. **A real publisher will never charge an author for anything, ever.** The great authors did not make money by paying their publisher. They made money by getting paid by their publisher. Stephen King does not pay his publisher. Stephen King's publisher pays him. The publisher makes money from the author through book sales in the form of royalties. If anyone claiming to be a publisher asks you for money or a fee, run. It is a scam. There are no exceptions to this rule.

4. **A real agent will never charge an author for anything, ever.** The great authors did not make money by paying their agents. A real agent gets paid by taking a percentage of royalties. The

HOW TO SELF-PUBLISH YOUR BOOK FOR FREE AND NOT GET CONNED

BY
#1 BESTSELLING AUTHOR
TW Robinson

DISCLAIMER:

All of the information in this publication is *MY
OPINION ONLY*. My opinion is based on my
experience and training as a self-published
author. Other opinions may vary.

Now that that's out of the way, it should keep all the
bastards trying to con self-published authors from suing me.

industry standard is 15%. Stephen King does not pay his agent. Stephen King's agent gets paid by getting a percentage of his royalties. The agent makes money when the book sells. If anyone claiming to be an agent asks you for money or a fee, run. It is a scam. There are no exceptions to this rule.

5. **A real marketing firm or marketer DOES NOT solicit authors.** A real marketing firm or marketer is never going to solicit you in any way by social media, message, phone, or text message, at a convention, or anywhere else. If you are being solicited by someone calling themselves a marketer, run. It is a scam. There are no exceptions to this rule.

6. **No person and/or entity can promise you a TV deal, a movie deal, a #1 bestseller, or anything else. NOTHING legit can be guaranteed, ever.** Run from anyone who tries to tell you they can hand you all of the hopes and dreams that every author has … for a fee. There are no exceptions to this rule.

KNOW THESE RULES. FOLLOW THESE RULES. DON'T GET CONNED.

Even if you are flat broke and have no money to spend on anything, you can be a successful self-published author. All you need is a computer, a program to write in, and access to the internet. That is it. A broke person usually can find these in a public library or with a friend.

You can write your book for free. You can edit your book for free. You can format your book for free. You can make a cover for your book for free. You can upload your book to major vendors for free. You can promote your book for free. You can get on all major bestseller lists for free. And you can make lots of money for free. You don't need anyone for anything if you learn the business. You don't have to have a paid copyright. You don't have to buy an ISBN. All you need is the know-how. You can learn to do all of this on the internet. The instructions and instructional videos are everywhere. If you don't know how to do it, you can learn how. Let me give you the basics in this book.

About the Author

Hello, everybody. I'm TW Robinson. I'm an Amazon #1 bestselling author. At the time I'm writing this book, I've been into self-publishing for a year and a half. I am just getting started myself. Here's the basic story of my career: I wrote a lot of stories, decided to turn them into a book, spent $75 to make it, and self-published it. It became a #1 bestseller in two Amazon categories. Want to know something funny? I was drunk when I wrote most of my book. I'm serious. I'll explain all that later in the chapter "How I Got Started in Self-Publishing."

One reason I am writing this brief book is, I have heard thousands of times, from thousands of people, that it is impossible to self-publish and make money or have any success. It's not true. I got drunk, wrote a book, and became a #1 bestseller by accident. If I can do that, anyone can do it if they really try, and if they follow the tried-and-true methods.

I'm a retired cop. When I was first hired as a police officer back in 1993, I didn't fill out an application, get hired, go to work, get a gun, a badge, a cop car, and a pat on the back with a smile and a "Have fun." They trained me. I went through two months of in-house training. I went to a three-month academy. I then spent almost four months riding with a training officer to put everything I had learned into practice. I was graded every step of the way. I also had to pass a written test, a physical test, and a psychological test.

I was trained to do my first job and was very successful at it. After I figured out how I got accidental success as an author, I decided to write books for a living. So I trained to do it. I have spent more than a year reading every article I can, watching every free webinar I have been offered, paid for expensive training on publishing and marketing books, and talked to many successful self-published authors who have made more than $1 million in the past decade selling their books at major online vendors without the "help" of an agent, publisher, or marketer of any kind.

I am sharing everything I have learned by experience and everything I have learned in those classes. The main reason I wrote this is that most of the people telling new authors they cannot make it are con artists posing as legit publishers. Being an ex-cop, I hate crooks. So allow me to prove those people wrong by explaining everything I can think of to help you get started.

After you read this book, I would suggest beginning your own writing career by going to the first place I started: Sarra Cannon, a very successful self-published author, has a YouTube channel called "Heart Breathings." She gives new authors great advice. Her videos are well labeled, to the point, and easy to understand, and she is an amazing teacher. She made more than $1 million as a self-published author after about a decade of writing. If you want to write a book or don't know what to do after you have written a book, start there. She also has two very good paid classes called "Publish and Thrive" and "HB90." I have taken both classes and they were well worth every cent I spent on them.

The purpose of this information is to prove to new authors that they can have successful careers without an agent or a publisher. I am not going to go into every single thing you would have to do at each step. I am going to show you the steps to take and point you in the right direction on how to take them.

Contents

CHAPTER 1
The Intro

Hello, ladies and gentlemen. In November of 2021, I posted on social media that there were way too many con artists looking to con new authors out of their money in a lot of Facebook author groups. These crooks are disguising themselves as publishers. Turns out, the administrators of many of those groups were not only allowing this behavior, but also encouraging it.

These people **are not** traditional publishers in any way, shape, form, or fashion. They are "vanity publishers." Vanity publishers are basically pretending to be publishers for the sole purpose of milking an author for as much money as they can get. They don't give a damn about the author or the author's book. You will **never** make any significant money paying these people. Ever.

Many are now calling themselves "hybrid publishers." Let me define that for you. A hybrid publisher is **the exact same thing** as a vanity publisher. I suspect they chose to use this name because there *is* such a thing as a hybrid author — an author who has both traditionally published books and self-published books.

You do not need a publisher to be a successful author these days. No author has needed a publisher of any kind for more than a decade now to make a great living as an author. Those days are gone. I know many authors who make six and seven figures a year without the help of these crooks or any real publisher. Many people may tell you it can't be done. They are lying, or they are wrong. I know it can. I publish without an agent or a publisher. I have made money and so have tons of others.

Let me be very clear on this. There is nothing these people can do for you that you cannot do for yourself. By that I mean, **nothing!** If you want to be an author, you do not need a real agent or a real publisher. And you certainly do not need someone pretending to be an agent or a publisher.

I am a #1 bestselling author. I chose to self-publish. I refuse to even talk to a publisher of any kind. I am also a retired police officer with a quarter of a century's worth of experience putting criminals in jail. I can spot a con a mile away. Every crook on social media who is soliciting new authors is doing so because they know that author has little to no understanding of how the publishing business works. These con artists are really taking advantage of that.

I got so tired of seeing these crooks posting on Facebook "Now accepting manuscripts." Some of them are even soliciting under the authors' public posts. So I offered to help anyone who had any problems, for free. And I meant that. Any new author or aspiring author who needs help, I am willing to help for free. Keep your money and spend it where it matters. But here's the problem.

I expected to get a dozen or so messages when I posted my offer. As of right now, I have received 432 messages from authors asking for help. I have spent the majority of my days answering questions, looking at books and blurbs, and giving advice. I am so far behind that I just can't get to all of them. I never expected that kind of response. I am glad to help, but with 432 messages, and replying to questions on the original posts, I just can't keep up. So here's how I am going to handle it. I am writing this book.

As an author who supports other authors, I'm here to support you. I am going to start at the very beginning. I am going to go through the steps of becoming a successful self-published author. I am going to tell you everything that I did. I am going to include what I did correctly. I am also going to include every time I screwed up. I am going to share what I have learned from some of the best in the business and from the training I took over the last year. I will also tell you where to get the same training if you want to take it yourself.

We are all authors. I do not for one second think that we are in competition with each other. Most readers buy dozens of books every year. Some buy hundreds. There is no reason we all can't make a good living writing books.

If you'd like a step-by-step instruction manual, here it is. I spent $75 on my book. That's it. Just $75. I made that back in two days. Again … #1 bestseller! I spent $75 on my book! You don't have to spend hundreds or thousands to do this. Anyone who tells you differently does not know what they are talking about or they are lying.

I am writing this small book and basically giving it away so authors who are looking at spending hundreds or thousands of dollars can save their money and be more successful staying away from social media vanity or hybrid publishers.

Do not misunderstand. I don't use the word "criminal" to describe these people. A criminal is someone who breaks the law.

Not all of these scammers are criminals. Let me give you a couple of definitions.

- **Con artist:** *A person who cheats or tricks others by persuading them to believe something that is not true.* This can be done legally.
- **Crook**: *A person who is dishonest or a criminal.* A person can be dishonest but not break the law.

Some of these vanity or hybrid publishers *are* breaking the law. But many are tricking new authors out of their money legally. I have seen a lot of websites that are basically telling new authors that they are going to screw them up front. These sites and con publishers literally tell authors they are going to charge thousands of dollars and keep royalties for things the authors could learn to do themselves in less than a week for free. There are thousands of sites like this just lying in wait for their next victim.

If the con publisher tells the author they will format the book for $1,000, put a cover on the book for $2,000, and edit and publish the book for another $2,000, and the author signs a contract, all the con has to do is format, cover, edit and publish the book for $5,000. Too bad the author didn't know they could get the book formatted for $50, get a cover designed for $50, do the editing themselves, and publish for free, save $4,900 and keep all their royalties.

For the most part, many vanity "publishers" are telling authors that for an astronomical fee, they will publish their books. The author pays up front and the vanity or hybrid publishers do exactly what I did myself for free. If you pay one of these publishers, and they do what they promise to do, they legally screw you.

In this brief book, I am going to prove to you that you can

do everything yourself if you are a new or aspiring author. You publish your own books. You keep all of your profits. You are in complete control of your work.

I cannot stress this enough. No legitimate person or publisher is going to sign an author they have never heard of for a book they have never read. It **ain't** happening. If you are approached, unsolicited, on social media by anyone claiming to be a publisher or agent, wanting *you* to pay *them* to be published, you are being conned, period.

There are no legitimate publishers where the author pays the publisher, ever! There are no exceptions to this rule. In the real world, in the real business, a real **publisher pays the author** … **ALWAYS!**

I am going to show you how you can do it on your own. In the last chapter I am going to show you how not to get conned by one of these fake publishers. Let's get started.

CHAPTER 2
How I Got Started In Self-Publishing

I retired from the Tuscaloosa Police Department at age 45 and started drawing a pension. When I would come home after having a beer with friends, I couldn't always just go to sleep. So I started writing down things that had happened during my career. I'd write short stories about things that I wanted to remember for the rest of my life.

I wrote about calls I had gone to, funny things other officers did on the job, pranks we played on each other, vacations we took, things we did at the bar, and many terrifying things that happened to us during our lives and careers. I wrote this stuff in my spare time for more than two years. I was almost always drinking when I wrote, just to pass the time. I was having fun. I never intended for anyone to ever read it other than myself, and I certainly had no intention of publishing it.

After two and a half years, I decided to get a job as a security guard at a local college. In addition to an application, they wanted a resume. I had worked every single year from age 16 to 45. Then there was a two-year gap without a job. I didn't think that looked good. So on a whim, I decided to turn what I had written over the past few years into a book. Then I could put "self-employed

— author" on my resume for the years that I had been retired without a job.

So I did. I created fake characters to do the things we had actually done in real life. I based all the main characters on real people. I used a real bar in my real hometown as the setting for the story with permission from the owner of that bar.

I decided that I would make it as interesting a read as I could, so I wrote a twist ending to the story. Creating this book was the most fun I had ever had. But I was planning to be a security guard, not an author. So I went the easiest route I could to getting the book published.

I wrote my own story. My wife, a copy editor by trade, edited the book. Then I paid a guy $75 to format my book in EPUB for my ebooks and PDF for my paperbacks. I took the picture for the cover myself. I looked up the directions on how to self-publish and uploaded my book to Amazon Kindle Direct Publishing, which is Amazon's self-publishing platform. On my private Facebook page, I posted in January 2020 that I was writing a book. I posted that I had finished it in May. I posted that it was being edited in June and would be out by August. On August 3, 2020, I posted it was out, along with the Amazon link where it could be bought. That is it. That is literally all I did.

Let me be clear: I did not hire an agent. I did not hire a publisher of any kind. I did not take out any ads. I did not do a book launch. I did not do any interviews. I did not do any podcasts or TV shows. I did not do anything at all other than post to fewer than 500 friends on a private Facebook page. That's it, folks. Nothing more.

I didn't even expect to sell a dozen copies. Why? Because I was told that's about how many I would sell. I was told I had to get an agent and a publisher and spend thousands of dollars to make money. **Bullshit**. Here's what happened:

On Monday, August 3, 2020, my book went up for sale on Amazon. On Tuesday, August 4, 2020, I had sold about a dozen copies. On Wednesday, August 5, 2020, less than forty-eight hours later, my book was a #1 bestseller in two categories, "Comic, Drama, and Plays" and in "New Releases."

Now, how in the hell did that happen? I got drunk, wrote a book, published it, and stumbled rear-end backward over a #1 bestseller on Amazon. I did not understand how it happened. So I started doing research because I had just done something that so many told me was not possible.

By the way, if you are going to be an author, do your research *before* you write your book. I had no idea that there was a tried, tested, and true way to write successful novels and publish them yourself. There is a scientific method for success. I did just enough by accident to make a little money and become a bestseller. I'm still not where I want to be, yet. I only got a taste. And I loved it.

When I did my research and saw how much money I could make by doing what I had a blast doing, I dropped the security guard job application and decided to be an author.

After more than a year's worth of training, I now know how it works and have shifted my way of doing things. I have traded my alcohol for coffee and now I am taking it seriously.

I will show you how to do what I did and how the major successful self-published authors do it. I'm going to start by giving you tips on writing your book.

CHAPTER 3
Writing Your Book

You have to have a good story that people want to read. If you don't have a good story, no matter what you do next, your book will not sell. It just won't happen. People are far more likely to write a one-star review if they don't like a book than they are to write a five-star review if they do like it. So write a good story. It's essential.

I suggest doing your research BEFORE you write. I did not do that. Here are a few facts that I wish I had known before I wrote my first novel. These facts would have been easy to find out. There's no telling how much more money I could have made if I had known the following (these figures are approximate but have been about the same for the last ten years):

- About **30%** of the books **published** every year are **fiction**.
- About **70%** of the books **published** every year are **nonfiction**.

In contrast ...

- About 75% of the books **bought** every year are **fiction**.
- About 25% of the books **bought** every year are **nonfiction**.

Also:

- Women buy 70% to 75% of all books purchased every year.
- Women buy fiction books for the most part.
- Men buy nonfiction books for the most part.
- The top bestselling genres in fiction are psychological thrillers, sci-fi and romance.
- A series of three or more books will make the most money of books sold in the indie author world, and a series is easier to market than a stand-alone novel.

So from a business point of view, your best bet is to write a psychological thriller, sci-fi, or romance, and make it a series. Also, write the story as if you were telling it to a 35-year-old soccer mom. That is who will most likely be buying your book.

However, I would not suggest writing something you don't like just because the genre or trope is popular. Write what you love. There will be a market for it. It will just take more time and effort to get less popular genres and nonfiction books to the right readers.

Nonfiction books can be successful. But it takes longer to climb the ladder of success with those. That is what I've heard in every class I have taken in marketing books. This is the only nonfiction book I ever plan to write. I have no firsthand experience with this.

Here's what I did right, by accident.

My book falls under the genre of literary fiction. It contains crime, drama, and some comedy, with a touch of thriller. Literary fiction is one of the better selling genres. (I did not know that when I wrote my book.) I released my book on Monday, August 3, 2020. Fiction books sell better in the months of August and

September. They also sell better on Mondays and Tuesdays. (I did not know that when I published my book.) You should never release your book when a popular author is releasing their book in the same genre as you. No popular author released their book in my genre the week before, during, or after my release. (I did not know that when I published my book.) Did you know that if a book hits the top ten list of bestsellers, it sells five times more copies than if it doesn't? Yeah. I didn't know that either.

If you go the self-publishing route, you aren't just an author, you are a business owner. That means you have to market your product. The key to success is marketing that product to the right customer. You can't just post a link to your book on promotion sites and expect it to sell. It won't. (I do have experience in this.) Those sites are full of authors. I posted my book link on many author promotion sites. Know who doesn't buy books often? Authors! I did not see one bit of difference in my sales after posting to dozens of Facebook promo sites. And I wasn't surprised.

I screwed up by not marketing my first book. I did not take out one single ad. I did not make any public appearances. I did not do any promotion of any kind. All I did was post on my private Facebook page that I was writing a book. Then, that I was about to release a book. Then, that it was available on Amazon and here's the link. That is all I did and it became a #1 bestseller. After the sales started dropping, then I tried out those free book promo pages on Facebook.

I based my book on a real police department, in a real town, at a real bar, and on real people. Many officers who still work at or had worked at the department bought it. Many people bought it because it was based on a town they either live in or once lived in. Some people who are regulars at or had been regulars at the bar bought it. Several family members the characters were based on bought it. Then, because it was a good story, their friends and family started posting it on their social media with a link, and many of their friends and family bought a copy. I also got several five-star reviews. (I did not solicit the reviews. I had no idea they were coming.) So that's how it snowballed into selling so many copies. It is still selling today, just not as well.

I have learned a lot in the past year. I look at being an author as a business. So I decided to look at it from a business perspective. I did research. One of the top selling genres is romance. The top selling subgenre in romance is erotic romance. (Think "Fifty Shades of Grey.") The top tropes in romance are contemporary, small town, and friends to lovers.

Finding all this out, I decided to write erotic romance exclusively from now on, with contemporary, small town, and friends to lovers tropes. Since I also found out that you do best when you write what you love, I am doing that too. I love to write about things that really happened to friends, family, and me. But since nonfiction doesn't sell as well, I am creating fictional characters who do what friends, family and I have done in real life and writing these events as fictional stories. I am having a blast doing it.

If you want to be a writer, WRITE. The first draft is probably going to suck. But you can edit it. Then edit it again. Then edit it again, until it doesn't suck. A well-known author, Jodi Picoult, once said, "You can always edit a bad page. You can't edit a blank page." I have found it is true. So write. That is the key.

If you aren't sure how to write a book, do an internet search. Seriously. Just search "How to write a book." You can go to

YouTube and do the same search and find thousands of videos. Some are good. Some suck. Some of the best videos are from Sarra Cannon, Hugh Howey, Jenna Moreci, and Alessandra Torre. Those are my go-to's if I need to look up advice. They are all six- and seven-figure-a-year authors. They all have way too many good videos to link here. So just do your own search and follow their advice. That is what I am doing. The YouTube Reedsy channel has good advice as well.

Here's something many indie authors don't know that *really* pisses off some traditionally published authors: Anyone can get on the major bestseller lists. That is correct. Self-published authors can make the New York Times bestseller list, The Washington Post bestseller list, The Wall Street Journal bestseller list, and the Amazon bestseller list just like traditionally published authors. You can be right beside Stephen King or J.K. Rowling on a list. All you have to do is write a good book, publish it, and market it correctly. (I'll get into all of that later.) So … write.

CHAPTER 4
Editing For Free And For Less

After you write your book, what comes next? Editing it. This **is not** where you want to skimp on price. It's one of the most important parts of this process, and hiring a professional editor can be well worth the cost. I generally would never recommend editing your own book. But if you *don't* have the money, there are ways to self-edit that can put your manuscript into pretty good shape. I'll list the five steps for free self-editing first. Then I'll go into things you can do for cheap editing. I'll also tell you how not to be taken by someone claiming to be an editor.

So, first, if you have no editing budget …

THE FREE SELF-EDITING WAY:

1) **Give your book a developmental edit.** This is where you bring your writing alive. Read through your book. Make your writing more powerful by removing all unnecessary words, such as "so," "but," "however," and "just." Remove any filler words that clutter your story. *Show* the reader what is going on instead of *telling* the reader what is going on. For example, don't say, "She was sad and started crying." Instead you could say, "She felt a burning in the pit of her stomach as her

breathing quickened. As tears began to fall, she lowered her head and brought her trembling hands to her face." If your character is running, mention how out of breath he is getting and how the wind is hitting his face. This also would be a good time to make it start raining so your character can step into puddles. Things like that. Look at the entire structure of your story, not just the sentences and words. Is there something you can add to the story to make it better? Are there parts that lag and need to be removed? Are the characters consistent? Are there any plot holes? Bring your reader into the action. When you are sure that everything is the way you want it, it is time for the next step.

2. **Line edit your manuscript.** Go through what you have written one sentence at a time — but not from beginning to end. Edit the last sentence of your book first. Then edit the sentence before that one, then the sentence before that. Work your way backward to the first sentence in your book. This will force you to stay focused on the editing instead of reading your story. Your mind will play tricks on you if you don't. Your brain will see what you *meant* to write instead of what you actually *did* write. You can miss a lot when you are editing your book front to back. You'll be amazed how many more errors you catch if you edit it from back to front.

3. **Use a free electronic editor.** There are a ton of paid programs that claim to make your writing better. Some authors swear by them. Some say they are useless and that mistakes still get through. I've never used one. I don't see a reason to buy one. Some of those things cost several hundred dollars. What I have done is load portions of my manuscript into a Gmail message. Hit "compose" and paste one paragraph at a time into the

message. Gmail will automatically underline all misspellings in red. It will outline other errors in blue. If you hover over the underlined area, it will make recommendations on how it should be changed. Not all of its recommendations will be correct, but most will. Gmail will keep your tense correct and will suggest changes such as "your" instead of "you're" and "to" instead of "too." The cool thing is, it is free. There are also several free editors online if you'd like to search for one.

4. **Drop your text into a text-to-speech program.** After you're done with the electronic editor, listen to the text of your book. A quick internet search will show you several free text-to-speech programs. Use the one you like best. (I use natural-readers.com.) If a mistake has made it through the first three steps, it likely will stick out like a sore thumb when you hear a voice read it to you. You also can read your book aloud to yourself as an additional step if you'd like.

5. **Now read your book.** See if you can spot any mistakes. If you do, correct them. Then comes the fun part. Wait one week without touching or even looking at your book and do it all again. Keep repeating the process weekly until you stop finding mistakes. When you can go through this entire process without finding anything wrong, you are done. As an additional step, you might find a friend to read through your manuscript for free and see if they find any mistakes. This will take a long time. But it is free and well worth the time if you don't have a budget.

You might even form an alliance with other writers. If you are good at finding continuity errors and beta reading, you could beta read another author's book for free. In return, if that author is good at grammar, they might edit your book for free. You'd save money on an editor, and they would save money on a beta reader. If you can assemble a group of several authors, you could copyedit each other's work for free. It took a while, but I now have an alliance with several other authors. We help each other.

Now, say you have a little (but not much) money to spend ...

EDITING ON A SLIGHTLY LESS LIMITED BUDGET:

1) **Consider someone other than a professional book editor.** If you do have some money to pay an editor, but not a lot, I would *not* recommend looking online for a professional book editor. These people charge an arm and a leg. I have heard many authors claim to have paid thousands of dollars for an editor. I'd never do that. I would recommend contacting your local middle school or high school, maybe even a local college, and trying to find an English teacher or professor to pay for help. Educators usually love to read and may be more than willing to edit your book for a modest fee. I have heard of them doing it for $20 an hour. You also might look for a current or former copy editor at a newspaper or magazine in your hometown. Why pay a professional book editor $75 an hour to do the same thing an English teacher or copy editor would be willing to do for $20? The English teacher may even be better at it than many of these expensive wanna-be's on social media.

Many people have disagreed with me on this. Some have gotten angry — and been very rude — that I even suggested it. Guess what their profession is? If you guessed an editor, you'd be right. Isn't it funny how that works? They will say things like, "An editor knows the style in which a book should be written… an editor knows the act structure. An author don't know these things." Well, the author could know these things. The author could just look it up on the internet for free. That's what I did. Many editors do not want you doing anything other than hiring them. But it can be done with success, especially when you are just starting out and just **do not** have the money. When you have made enough money, then I would recommend hiring an industry professional.

2. **Know how to hire the best, without getting taken.** Let's say you do choose to hire a professional book editor. The easiest and safest way to do this is to ask reputable authors for recommendations. Many well known authors will respond to you if you reach out to them for something like this.

   Now let's say you don't have any recommendations and you're considering someone who claims to be an industry professional editor. Before you pay someone to edit your book, ask for a sample edit. Pay the person to spend one hour editing part of your manuscript. See how they do. But for Pete's sake, if someone says, "Hey, I'm an editor," don't give them your book, pay them $3,000 and say, "Have at it!" That is just bad business.

   With all the crooks trying to rip off new authors, it is worth checking out everything, including those who claim to be industry professional editors. Ask them for references. Then **check** the references they give you. Ask them which books they have edited. Check out the books. Oh yeah, another great way to be sure who edited a book is to check with the author. Some people will lie about being a good editor and what they have done. Can you believe that?

3. **Remember why you're doing this step.** Most readers are willing to overlook a few mistakes. But they won't overlook a lot. If you don't polish up your grammar as much as possible, your reader may very well put your book down and give you a one-star review.

When readers see an error, it takes them out of the story. You certainly don't want that. Chances are, your book will not be perfect. Many traditionally published New York Times bestselling books contain a few errors. I have seen those errors myself. I have seen a character's name misspelled. I have seen continuity errors. I have seen a character call another character by the wrong name. I have seen sentences that did not start with a capital letter in many traditionally published books. The goal is to have no errors. But at least try to have as few as possible.

Again, if you just don't have the money for an editor, do the free stuff to start out. You can always pay to have your book edited when you make money. Don't put your dreams on hold for years just because people tell you that you *need* an editor. You don't. Many millionaire self-published authors started out doing this.

WHAT I DO:

On my books, I do all the listed steps above for free self-editing. Then I give my manuscript to a friend who teaches English (with an English degree). After she is done, I give it to my secret weapon … my wife. I am lucky that I am married to a copy editor by trade. She has degrees in English, journalism, and communications. She has been in the newspaper business for more than twenty-five years. She was in charge of the copy desk in her newsroom for more than a decade. She now does planning for three newspapers at a big company. She also edits books on the side. She is amazing. Nothing gets past her. (FYI, she doesn't edit my social media posts. That is all me, misspellings, poor grammar and all.) My English teacher friend is also an author. So I beta read for her in return for her line editing.

My next chapter will be on formatting. It will be short because I *suck* at formatting. That's what I have to pay for. I hate to do it. I tried to learn, but I have no interest in it. I pay a guy less than $100 to do all the formatting I need. But I'll tell you what all the experts say to do and I'll let you know what you probably shouldn't do.

CHAPTER 5
Formatting Your Book

This isn't going to be a long chapter.

WHAT I DO:

I hire someone to format my books. The end. (Frowning face.)

There is nothing I can teach you or help you with when it comes to formatting. I don't know much about it.

WHAT I KNOW:

Here's what little I do know about formatting, if it helps in any way.

Almost every author I have talked to uses Microsoft Word or Scrivener for formatting.

Every major vendor requires the following formats: An EPUB file is needed to publish your book in ebook form, and a PDF file is needed to publish your book in paperback form. I do not have any published hardbacks or audiobooks yet. I also have never published anything with pictures or illustrations. (Even though there is a picture in this book, it hasn't been formatted at the moment I am writing this.) I have gotten dozens of messages asking me how to go about formatting a children's book. I don't have an answer. Sorry. But I can point you in the right direction for all of the above.

You can use the website Fiverr.com to connect with thousands of people who do freelance work for authors. It is free to join and you have no obligations. You pick the services you need a la carte. There are freelancers who ghostwrite, edit, format every kind of book there is, design covers, design ads, make audiobooks, beta read, etc. (Be careful when hiring someone to ghostwrite a book for you. Some have been caught plagiarizing.)

I joined Fiverr after another author recommended it. Everyone who does work on the site has the following: a list of examples of their work, their rates for said work, and a rating system of up to five stars and reviews on authors who have used them. The freelancer cannot change or edit the ratings or reviews. That part is owned by Fiverr. The reviews you see are real reviews.

To get started, go to the section for formatters. Pick the style you want and message the freelancer. Tell them what you need and when you need it. After a brief chat, you submit an order form that is very specific to your needs. Then you wait to hear back from the freelancer. (This usually takes a few days.) The freelancer will put the work you asked for into a program that will let you view the finished product. You can't use the work yet. You view it and either accept it as is or ask for changes. (I have never heard of a freelancer who wouldn't make changes you need for free.)

After you view the work, now, and *only now*, do you pay for it. You pay the site, and the freelancer is paid for the work. You then download the EPUB and PDF files you need. You're done. If you are happy, keep the information about the freelancer that you used. *Never* pay for the work until you see it and approve it. My opinion is it should always be that way; I'll never pay for something I don't approve first.

The charges for formatting start at about $30 and increase depending on your needs. I chose a guy who did both EPUB and PDF files. I'd recommend using someone who does both. My book is 222 pages long and almost 58,000 words. I paid $75 for the services.

Many people over the past year have advised me never to use Fiverr. I have seen this posted in every author-related social media site that I have been on. When I started looking at all the people who said this, I noticed the overwhelming majority were people who did work exactly like you can get on Fiverr. The big difference was they typically charged way more for their work and insisted on being paid up front. Funny, eh? You should be seeing a pattern develop by now.

That is all I have for you on formatting.

Next I will talk about covers and designing.

CHAPTER 6
Covers

I know there is an old saying, "Never judge a book by its cover." Well, you can bet your behind that everyone does it anyway. Covers are another place where you do not want to cut corners. As with editing, you should never design your own cover … unless you just don't have the money. The better the cover, the higher your sales. If you can afford to hire a professional cover designer, do it. If you can't afford it, the tips below will help if you are just starting out.

Whether it's a physical copy in a bookstore or a thumbnail on an online vendor site, the book cover is the first thing that people will see. It should make potential customers want to pick up the book or click on the thumbnail and read about it. This is the very first step in what you hope will result in a sale. Remember, your cover is one of the most important marketing tools you have.

Your cover should clearly convey to the reader your book's genre and what it is about. I suggest going to Amazon and looking at all covers of the bestselling books in your genre. This is not the time to get artistic and go out on a limb. The cover is for the reader, not you.

WHAT I DO:

The first thing I do is brainstorm what I want on the cover. I look at all the bestselling covers in my genre. Then, I take my own photos for the covers for my books.

I plan to do this for the foreseeable future. The reason I take my own pictures with my own camera is that a professional cover designer uses tons of stock photos to make book covers. If you do this, you don't own the picture on your cover. You just have permission to use it. And so will others. I once heard a very successful self-published author say that the image used on the cover of her bestselling novel was used on sixteen other books that she knew about. I hate the thought of that. So I take my own pictures. That way, I can copyright my cover image when I copyright my book. It will be unique to me and my book only. I was looking through a list on Amazon of erotic romance covers and saw the same stock image on three different books ... by three different authors.

My first novel was about a group of police officers who meet at a local bar at night to celebrate their friend and co-worker's twenty-five years with the department. The overall tone of the story is dark. So one Tuesday after midnight, I took a picture of the entrance to the real-life bar where my story takes place. I then put it into a program and manipulated the picture to match the genre and tone of my book. I've had a lot of experience and I knew I was able to do it.

You can see the difference in the real bar and my book cover below. My friend Brooks Barksdale took this photo of himself holding up my book cover as he stands in front of the bar, in the daytime, in the same place I stood to take my original photo for the cover.

I have heard of people being charged up to $5,000 for a cover. That is beyond ridiculous to me, especially since there are people who do a great job for only $100. You can get custom-made covers starting at $25 on Fiverr (the website I mentioned in the last chapter). They are cheap, but many are fine for an author just starting out. Also, when you start making money, you can always  go back and hire a professional to change the cover to something better. For example, Sarra Cannon has changed the covers on the books in her "Shadow Demons" saga three times.

If you just don't have any money to spend on covers, there are other *free* routes to take. For example, you can create your own cover in a graphic design platform called Canva. You also can design your own cover in Amazon's Kindle Direct Publishing platform. It provides authors a free, easy-to-use template. Also, keep it simple if you don't have much or any experience. It's better to have a good simple cover than a bad complex one.

Since I came up with my own way at the very start, my cover design experience probably won't fit many authors' needs. So here are a few tips I got from an author I trust. She made some comments on a post I made a few days ago. I won't embarrass her by calling her name. But her initials are H.M. Brandon. (Smiley face.)

She said that she uses Canva in tandem with Cooltext.com for color fonts. She also recommended GetCovers.com, which is a sister site of MiblArt book cover design company. It looks pretty cool and there are some great-looking cheap covers there. Some start at $5 for ebooks. There's a package for ebooks and print covers for only $25. Apparently, the cover designers on the site also offer unlimited changes.

There are plenty of legit people online who are great cover designers. You can find several people on Facebook who can make great covers for you at an affordable price. But vet them before you use them.

There are plenty of people just starting out who suck at it and try to pass themselves off as industry professionals. **Beware.** Do your research before you hire anybody for anything. If they don't have examples of covers they have done, if they don't have a social media presence such as a website or Facebook page, and if they can't be easily located and contacted, as author H.M. Brandon said, "Run the other way."

There also are many possibilities for affordable cover designers on Fiverr.

Just remember that for print books, you'll need to know how many pages you have so you know how big to make the spine of the book. Your book *must* be formatted before you create your cover.

I have had several people tell me that nobody should ever design their own covers. They have been downright rude on some of my social media posts. Do you know what most of them do for a living? If you guessed that they design covers, you win a cookie. (I'm not really giving you a cookie.)

Seeing that pattern yet?

Up next are copyrights and ISBNs, which might sound complicated but really aren't.

CHAPTER 7
Copyrighting and ISBNs

ISBNs and copyrights are two different things, and have nothing to do with each other. I am putting them in the same chapter because both lessons are so short.

While it's a good idea for an author to get copyrights and ISBNs, you don't absolutely have to do either. You have to pay for both and if you have no money to do it, then you don't have to do these steps to publish. In the United States, the copyright is yours as soon as you write the book, and ISBNs are needed if you're going to sell your book in stores or on multiple online vendors that do not supply them for you (more on that later).

ABOUT ISBNs:

An International Standard Book Number is a thirteen-digit identifier unique to each book or version of that book. The books that require an ISBN are paperbacks, hardcovers, and audio-books. Ebooks *do not* require an ISBN.

Most vendor sites will give you a free ISBN if you publish with them, but consider your options before you decide whether to go this route.

On the plus side, just because these sites automatically give you an ISBN does *not* mean that they own the rights to your book. You own the rights to your work unless you give away or sell the rights to another entity … like, say, a *real* traditional publisher or a *fake* vanity publisher out to screw you.

Many self-published authors do not buy ISBNs for their books. They use the free ones that are provided by the vendor. You could do the same thing and just leave it at that.

However, you can't use that ISBN anywhere except for on that site. There are advantages to buying your own.

If you decided to publish to a wider audience, or to use a publishing platform like IngramSpark to distribute your book, you would need your own ISBN. Make sure you know the vendor's rules. There are too many to list here. Do an internet search, go to the vendor, and read the rules for yourself. I'll leave that up to you.

Also, if you publish your book in different formats, then the paperback, audiobook, and hardcover all require different ISBNs. So does the ebook format, if you choose to use an ISBN on it (remember, an ISBN is not required for ebooks).

Here is what ISBNs cost the last time I checked, about three months ago:

1 ISBN - $125

10 ISBNs - $295

100 ISBNs - $575

1,000 ISBNs - $1,500

You need to get your ISBN from the official provider in your country. For example, the only place you can get an ISBN in the United States is from Bowker, a company based in New Jersey.

Do not buy an ISBN from anywhere else. An ISBN is not transferable. Run from a "publisher" who says they will provide your ISBN. (NOTE: A vendor like Amazon KDP that supplies them for free *is not* a publisher.)

Here is where you would request and pay for your own ISBN, along with direct links to their ISBN services:

- **If you're in the United States:** Bowker

https://www.myidentifiers.com

- **If you're in Canada:** Library and Archives Canada

https://www.bac-lac.gc.ca/eng/news/videos/Pages/isbn-canada.aspx

- **If you're in Sweden:** National Library of Sweden

https://www.kb.se/isbn-och-utgivning/isbn.html

You'll have to look up the others yourself if you live in a country other than the three listed above.

Your own ISBN will also help if your self-published book ends up in bookstores like Barnes & Noble. Yes, that is possible! I'll tell you how in the marketing lesson. And, no, you do not need a publisher or an agent to get your book into a major retailer like Barnes & Noble or Walmart. You can do it yourself. Bet your crook vanity publisher never mentioned that, did they?

ABOUT COPYRIGHTS:

If you're in the United States, the *only* place to get your copyright is from the U.S. Copyright Office.

https://www.copyright.gov

There are many other websites that offer to sell you copyrights. Don't do it.

These other sites exist solely because people know that new authors do not know the business, and they are taking advantage of that. They also could be getting the copyrights for themselves and not for the author. If that happens, it is a whole new can of worms. But, hey, if you like getting screwed over, go for it.

If you don't live in the U.S., you'll have to do an internet search to find out where you need to get or buy your copyrights. Sorry. I can't help you there. I have been told the United Kingdom and Canada will provide them for free.

There is way too much info on copyrights to put here. You'd still be reading this chapter next week if I were to write it all. If you have any questions, 99% can be answered here:

https://www.copyright.gov/help/faq/index.html

Here is the most important information. The minute you write a novel, you own the copyright to it. You are not required to get any written work copyrighted. It is automatically yours if you write it. That is the law in the U.S. If you don't have money to spend, you don't need to get your work copyrighted. However, I recommend getting your books copyrighted anyway if you can afford it.

Not only does the copyright give you a license from the federal government saying that the work belongs to you, but it is also easier to get your books removed from somewhere if they are ever pirated by someone else. I get everything I do copyrighted. And guess what? My book did get pirated after it became a #1 bestseller. I found it on a site where I did not publish it. This is a real concern even for self-published authors. (My book is no longer pirated. It was removed.)

But here is the big reason I get everything copyrighted. I do it in case someone else claims that *I* stole *their* work. Having a copyright in your back pocket stops false claims then and there. (I know this from the days when I played in a band and we released albums. We got all of our original music copyrighted.)

Here is another fun-filled fact about copyrights. I took a class several months ago on marketing books. One of the lessons was on copyrights. That's where I learned most of this information. The class cost $450. I know. A lot, right? Not really.

I say not really because I thought, as did everyone else in the class, that you had to pay for a copyright on every single book that you wrote. I found out that if you publish your ebook first and do get a copyright on it, that ebook copyright extends to all other versions -- paperback, hardback, audiobook, etc. However, If you publish a paperback or any other form of your book before you get a copyright on your ebook, you have to get every other version of your book copyrighted. So for Stephen King's sake, get a copyright on your ebook *first, before* you publish it in any other way. By the way, ebook copyrights are cheaper. So that information saved me from buying many extra copyrights that I didn't need to buy. But wait! It gets better.

The twelve books I am writing now are a series. You can copyright an entire series for one price — the price of one ebook. In that $450 class I found out that I had to pay for just one ebook copyright because my books were all part of one series, so even after paying for that class, I saved more than $800! If I had not taken the class, I would have paid $1,250 for copyrights. Now I am going to pay $35. That's it. The moral of the story is it pays to train yourself in your profession.

Being an author is a profession. If you are an author, you are a business owner. Save money where you can. The more you know, the more you will save. This is all general knowledge; train yourself beyond what I am giving you here.

That's all I have for ISBNs and copyrights.

Now for the big one... *publishing*. I'll tell you how to publish your book, for free, without an agent or publisher. After the step of publishing, you're done with the hard stuff. Your book can now earn you a passive income for the rest of your life.

CHAPTER 8
Publishing Your Book

This is where new authors are taken advantage of the most. For some reason, many authors or aspiring authors actually believe they need a publisher to be successful. They don't. But because they think they do, they go looking online and end up signing away their books, their rights, their profits and everything else to con artists who can't wait to screw them over.

I'll say it again. No legitimate publishers are going to sign an author they have never heard of nor are they going to sign that author because of a book they have never read, **ever.** No legitimate publishers are soliciting authors on social media. There are no exceptions to these rules. Publishers who ask you for any amount of money **are** crooks. They may be about to take all of your money legally, but they are still, by definition, crooks. Legal and right have nothing to do with each other. Illegal and wrong are not related either.

A true publisher pays an author. An author will **never** pay a **real** publisher for anything. An author does not pay a publisher for editing. An author does not pay a publisher for covers. An author does not pay a publisher for formatting. An author does not pay a publisher for an ISBN. An author does not pay a publisher for copyrights. An author does not pay a publisher for publishing. An author does not pay a publisher for **anything**. A publisher pays for all of these things up front, then recovers these expenses before the author is paid. Then the author and publisher split the royalties.

Let me give you a few stats that I found on AuthorEarnings.com. In 2016, self-published authors earned almost 70% of their royalties from their vendors, according to the site, while traditionally published authors with small, legitimate publishers made around 35% of their royalties. Authors signed to the "Big 5" publishers made less than 20% of their royalties overall.

If you go the traditional publishing route, you will have zero access to your sales charts. They will be provided to you by your publisher. If you do everything yourself and self-publish, you have complete access to everything you sold and all the royalties you have earned. I'll give you an example.

If I had signed with a real publisher, I would not have the password for the vendor sites where my book was sold (in my case, Amazon). My publisher would just tell me what I sold and how much money I made. Amazon would pay my publisher my royalties. The publisher would take their cut, then send me a check for the rest. I'd just have to take their word for what I made and sold. I'd have to assume the charts and figures they provided to me were real.

However, I self-published. That means I have access to my Amazon account. I can sign in and see how many books I sold and how much money I made. All of my royalties are direct deposited into my business account. I don't have to ask anyone a damn thing or take anyone at their word, and I keep *all* of the profits. Nobody else puts their hands on my money or into my bank account. There's no way I am giving up that freedom.

Since 2016, according to AuthorEarnings.com, there are far more successful self-published authors than traditionally published authors who are making a full-time career of writing books. In fact, according to the site, there are almost three times as many successful indie authors as traditionally published authors making more than $50,000 a year. Stephen King, J.K. Rowling, John Grisham, and Anne Rice are exceptions in traditional publishing. They are not the rule. More than 90% of traditionally published authors still have a day job because they don't make enough to support themselves on book royalties alone.

Now, welcome to the part that makes reading all this stuff worthwhile. Let's get into how to do this for yourself, without help from an agent or publisher, real or otherwise.

HOW TO PUBLISH YOUR BOOK:

1. Create an account at the vendor where you would like to sell your books (for example: Amazon KDP).
2. Follow their fairly easy directions.
3. Fill out all the blanks that apply to you and your book.
4. Upload your covers.
5. Upload your EPUB and PDF files.
6. Select a payment method for your royalties. This will be a check or direct deposit.
7. If direct deposit, fill in the account info where it is to be deposited.
8. Click "Done" and wait.

9. Within twelve to seventy-two hours, your book will either be approved or not.
10. If your book is not approved, make the needed changes. (Usually this is because you forgot to fill in a blank.)
11. If your book is approved, look over your ebook proof to make sure it's to your liking.
12. If you have a paperback, ask the vendor to send the author proofs to make sure everything is to your liking.
13. If all is good, then click "publish."

This, in a nutshell, is how all the major vendors work. Each vendor has instructions on how to upload your book. There are also many videos on YouTube showing how to upload to every vendor listed here and then some. By the way, some vanity publishers will charge you hundreds or thousands of dollars to publish your book on Amazon alone. I had no clue how to do it myself. The day I published my book, I started watching videos and reading directions about 9 a.m. and was done and published before noon.

You're done! Congratulations! You are now just as published as if you were signed to a traditional publisher. You are now just as published as Stephen King! Everything his publisher does for him at a high price and for more than half of his royalties, you just did yourself for free.

Here's the cool thing. If you did all of this yourself and you didn't use a publisher — vanity, hybrid or any other kind — your book and all the profits are yours and yours alone … forever. Your book will never go out of print. It will earn you money for the rest of your life.

You can get your books into every major online vendor by

yourself. If you sell enough books on Kobo's website, it is possible to get your books into stores like Walmart. If you sell enough books on Barnes & Noble's website, the Barnes & Noble store can sell your books on the shelf in their stores, even if you are self-published without an agent or publisher. I won't list the amounts you need to sell here because I want to keep this book valid as long as possible. The amounts you need to sell in order to do this may change over time. Do a search to keep up with the requirements.

SOME MARKETING BASICS:

Now that you know the general steps on how to publish your book, it's time to learn how to incorporate marketing into the process.

Market your book to the readers who are interested in your genre and you can start making money. (I'll show you how to do this later in a marketing lesson.) You are a self-publisher. You did this yourself. You haven't hired anyone so far. Do not hire anyone now either. You weren't taken by a con publisher or agent. There is no reason to be taken by a con marketer. And yes, they are out there. Thousands and thousands of them *are* out there.

Now, let me break this down into small steps you will need to do to get it right. I'm also going to tell you what information you will need while filling out the online forms during the publishing process.

I am going to tell you all about keywords, genres and blurbs. You will need all this information when you are publishing to all major vendors. I will use Amazon as the example in all of the following information. I know Amazon KDP better than I know any other vendor, and more people publish on Amazon than any other place. Other vendors will vary a bit. But not much.

KEYWORDS:

These are the words that the vendor is going to ask you to enter to help readers in your target audience find your book when they search your genre. Don't take this lightly. The words you enter here could be the difference in your book appearing at the top of the search results or at the end. So research what you need to put here. The closer you get to the top of the search results, the better your chances for a sale. The right words could help result in a New York Times bestseller. The wrong words (even if off a little bit) could result in virtually no sales at all.

These can be something like "small town" or "erotic" or "spicy" or "police," to give a few examples. However, the keywords or phrases should be based on *your* book's contents. If you wrote a horror novel, for example, you wouldn't want to put "outdoor cooking" in your keywords.

A program from Amazon KDP called Publisher Rocket helps with this step. I have heard a lot of great things about it. I have heard a few not-so-great things. I have seen example videos on YouTube. It looked very interesting. I have never used it myself. I'll do a review if I ever purchase it.

WHAT I DO:

I go to the search bar on Amazon and click on the Kindle department. Then I start typing things that I think would be related to my books. It will auto-populate the most popular search words at the moment, similar to how Google works. When I see a search term that pertains to my book, I use that word or phrase in my keywords. It's free to do this.

These searches can shift in popularity over time. A popular search word or phrase now may not be popular next month. I stay current. At the beginning of every month, I do the search again. If the popular search terms have changed, I change them in my keywords. You can go into your account and edit anything you have previously done, including your keywords.

Keep a list of all the keywords that you are currently using. You can take a screen shot of your keywords in your Amazon account so you can easily compare it the next time you do a keyword search.

GENRES:

Make sure you know what genre and subgenre your book falls into. Do your research. Each genre and subgenre has very specific rules that *must* be followed. If you put your book into a genre where it does not belong, it could result in bad reviews and discourage a reader from ever reading any of your future work. I'll give you an example.

In romance, the biggest rule is the couple *must* get together at the end and live happily ever after. Want to piss off a ton of romance readers? Market your book as a romance and kill off one of the characters at the end; don't have a happily ever after ending. There are romance readers out there who would be willing to kill you over that. While they may not actually kill you, they will give you a detailed one-star review in a heartbeat. So know your genre and the rules of your genre. There are too many to list. You can do an internet search to find tons of articles and videos explaining these in detail.

I'll give you my lists for my upcoming twelve-book series as an example:

My genre: romance

My subgenre: erotic (not to be confused with "erotica")

My tropes: friends-to-lovers, contemporary, small-town

I know exactly where I fit in. How do I know? Research. So any reader who sees my book will know that my book is a romance containing graphic sex scenes about friends who become lovers in modern times in a small town and they live happily ever after in the end. You will need to know this information about your book before you publish it. Don't get lazy and wing it. This is important. The more accurate you are, the higher the chance people who are interested will see your book. If it gets in front of the right eyes, it gets a sale. You make more money.

A great free tool to check other books' genres is on a website called NerdyBookGirl.com. Find a bestselling book that is similar to your story and do a search on what genres that book is in. If your story is similar enough, put your book in the same genres and subgenres. Pick a book that is a bestseller to model yours after. Here's the free link: https://nerdybookgirl.com/book-category-hunter/

BLURBS:

Your blurb is two to three paragraphs containing roughly two hundred words or less on the back cover of your book. It is also what you will list as the details beside your book on your vendor site to let potential readers know what your book is about.

Remember how your cover is also a marketing tool? So is your blurb. Your blurb is not just a description of your story, it is the most important marketing tool you have. Don't treat this lightly. Your cover got the potential customer's attention. Now they have clicked on the thumbnail of your cover and they are reading your blurb. This blurb is going to make their decision on whether to get out their credit card and give you money or go back to browsing.

There are several great videos about writing blurbs on YouTube. Watch a ton of these. Go to Amazon and see what the bestsellers similar to your book say in their blurbs. Now let me explain just how important your blurb is and how it can drastically help you or hurt you.

I was listening to a lecture from a very popular self-published author named Alessandra Torre. She has made millions selling her books. She said that one of the first books she self-published was doing all right. She was selling a few copies a day. It was nothing great. It had been available for a while. She decided to experiment. She did research and decided she would try a few different things, one at a time, to try to increase sales. The first thing she did was change her book blurb.

After she changed the blurb, that book's sales skyrocketed to a spot on the New York Times bestseller list. She made tons of money off it. All she did was change the blurb. By the way, if you have a publisher of any kind, you cannot change your blurb. Your publisher would have to do that for you, if they even approved. I bet many also would charge you for it.

So how do you know when you have spent enough time working on your blurb? Well, when you have pulled all of your hair out by the roots, your parents, children, spouse, and friends threaten to kill you if you start one more conversation beginning with, "How does this sound?" Then you will be ready to post it. If you haven't done that yet, you aren't done. (I exaggerate. But do spend time on it.)

The five major vendors are:

1. Amazon KDP (40% of all books bought in the U.S. are purchased on Amazon)
2. Apple Books
3. Barnes & Noble
4. Google Play Books
5. Kobo

Many indie authors choose to make a deal with Amazon KDP and sell their books only on Amazon by enrolling in a program called KDP Select. If you choose to do this, you cannot sell your ebook anywhere else in the world other than Amazon. You can't even give away your ebook on your website. The advantage of doing this is that Amazon then promotes your ebook over those of other indie authors who don't do this. Supposedly, your books come up faster and ahead of others in searches. I have been told this. I don't know for sure. Many authors have done this very thing and made millions. I plan to try it soon to see if it really works.

The other option is to "go wide." This means to sell your book everywhere you want and not be exclusive to anyone. There are advantages to this as well. One is that your book will be seen in more places by more potential readers.

Many authors did very well in KDP Select and then went wide and did better. Many authors did well wide and then went into KDP Select and did better. The results depend on where the most readers are who would enjoy your genre. I know an author who does better wide and I know an author who does better in KDP Select. The one who does better wide writes young adult paranormal books and romance novels. The author who does better in KDP Select writes murder and mystery series as well as nonfiction books. That's a big genre difference. Do research to find where your target readers are.

If you are on KDP Select, readers who sign up for Kindle Unlimited get to read your book for free. For the readers, it works kind of like Netflix does for movies and TV shows. When they read those books, the author gets paid for each page the reader clicks on. So it is possible to make money as an author if tons of people read your books yet never buy one. Amazon allows this feature only for KDP Select authors.

I have a lot of friends who write romance novels. So I'll give you an example of what I am doing.

I have chosen to write only romance from here on out. Because I am writing erotic romance with friends-to-lovers, small-town, and contemporary tropes, my target readers are females between the ages of 18 and 49. They are everywhere, not just Amazon. So my particular genre and subgenre has potential readers all over the internet. If I entered KDP Select, I would be missing the eyes of millions of potential customers. So it would not be wise for me, personally, to join that program and be exclusive to Amazon. I'm sure I could do well there. But I would miss a lot of my target audience. Research where your books would do better.

TERMS OF SERVICE:

I can't stress this enough: Each time you upload your book to a vendor, you will be asked to click "yes," that you have read the terms of service. So, actually *read* the terms of service. More importantly, follow them. If you don't, your book could get banned from the site. Or worse, *you* could get banned from the site. If you do get kicked off a major vendor site, it is possible that your self-publishing career could be hurt drastically. You may not be able to recover. Know what you can and cannot do.

Amazon has the strictest terms of service. There are a ton of things you are not allowed to use as keywords. Know them. Don't use them.

ADDITIONAL BLURB INFO:

You cannot use things like another author's name as a keyword on Amazon. You cannot use another author's title in your keywords on Amazon. You cannot use the word "bestseller" in your Amazon keywords. However, you can use all of those in your blurb.

Everything in your blurb is searchable when someone types into the search engine on Amazon, according to Amazon KDP expert Dave Chesson. But this can be tricky. Don't go to hash-tagging a bunch of words in your blurb that you can't use in your keywords. That looks tacky and desperate. I promise it will cost you sales.

When my book went to a #1 bestseller, I got to put "bestseller" in my blurb. Sales went up a bit. When a New York Times bestselling author gave me a good review, I quoted that author's review in my blurb. I also got to say who the quote was from and how important he was. Thus, I got to use the words "bestseller," the author's name, and his status as a "New York Times bestselling author" in my blurb. That is not against the terms of service. I can use those in my blurb, but not in my keywords. So I did. My sales went up a bit. (Thanks, Nick!)

ROYALTY RATES:

The way that you make money is by earning royalties from the vendor sites. The top vendor sites that I mentioned earlier pay the highest royalty rates. If you publish your book on all five (Amazon KDP, Kobo, Barnes & Noble, Apple Books, and Google Play Books) your average rate will be somewhere around 60% to 65% royalties. Most sites pay 70% while a few pay only 35% to 50%. (I can't remember which ones pay what. But you can look it up for yourself at each site.) The point is, if you self-publish, you get the most royalties and all the profits.

I have heard several people (none who are published) complain about this. I think it is a great deal. Consider something. Once you upload to their sites, you are done. You never have to spend more than a few days a year even thinking about that book. Each vendor site takes your orders, prints the book as soon as the order comes in, packages your book, and mails it to the customer. They also keep up with your royalties, pay you once a month, and send you a W2 at the end of the year for taxes. Print on demand is great as far as I am concerned. And they take less than half your royalties to do all this. I think it's a great deal.

THIS IS IMPORTANT:

What is your book worth? There are general guidelines at each vendor. But here is the real answer … and pay attention. Your book is worth *exactly* what people are willing to pay for it and *nothing more.* How much time you spent, how hard you worked, how long it is, how many words are used have nothing whatsoever to do with it. Your book is worth what people are willing to pay, period.

I'm sure you'd love to sell your book for $20. But if no one is willing to buy it for $20, it isn't worth that. But what if a million people would be willing to buy it for $8? I, personally, would set my book for $8 and sell a million copies rather than set it for $20 and not make anything. I have heard tons of authors argue over this. Many have refused to sell their book for less than *they think* it is worth. So they end up selling nothing. That is a bad business practice.

Now think about this. Many authors are just dying to get a deal with a real publisher. If they do manage to get signed by a legitimate small publisher, that publisher will do the same things, but they will usually take at least half of the royalties. Most of those signed to a small publisher can expect to see about 35% of what they earn.

Want to hear something even worse? Get signed by a Big 5 publisher. Those authors make only an average of 10% royalties on printed books and 25% royalties on ebooks. And as I said in an earlier chapter, the overwhelming majority of authors who are signed to a real publisher, big or small, don't make enough money to support themselves. They still have a day job.

If you self-publish, you get to keep all of your earnings. The vendor sites will take a cut of the royalties. But you were never going to get those royalties anyway. They take the same royalties from traditionally published authors who sell at the same vendors. If Amazon keeps 30% of your royalties for all the printing and paperwork they do for you, then your earnings are 70% of the royalties. That is your profit. I can't see myself sharing my profits with an agent and a publisher when I can do everything myself no matter how boring it is to accomplish.

Self-publishing your book is easy. You can advertise anywhere a traditional publisher can advertise. You can sell anywhere a traditional publisher can sell. You can do it all yourself and keep all the profits. It is easy. It is mind-numbing, time-consuming, and boring as hell to do at times. But it is easy. On Monday morning if you set out to self-publish your book and know nothing about publishing at all, you can research and start following directions. By Friday afternoon, you can be an expert.

Now let me tell you about how to make the money by marketing!

CHAPTER 9
Marketing Your Book

The number one reason self-published authors don't make money on their books (other than not writing a marketable book) is that they *don't try* to sell their books. They don't put in the time to do it. They don't know how to advertise. They fail to do what it takes to get their books in front of the eyes of customers who would be willing to buy it.

Just note, I am not an expert on this in any way. I have never run one single ad, ever. I got the following information from sitting through several book marketing classes, reading books by experts, and talking to very successful authors. This is the information that I used to plan my marketing strategy. This is where I spent the most money on classes. I have talked with numerous million-dollar-making authors on this topic. The information was great. I haven't tried any of this myself. But I do plan on it with my new series.

I have seen where it all worked via spreadsheets and receipts from authors who do it for a living. I wish I could share all the workbooks and worksheets I got from those classes. I can't because it would be unethical. It would be illegal in some cases because a lot of the material is copyrighted. I can tell you the gist of what I have learned (but have yet to apply).

FIRST OF ALL:

These will work only for your target audience. The goal is to get your book in front of people who will buy it. If you write horror novels, you want your book in front of people like Stephen King's fans, *not* those who read Christian romance. If you are writing a Christian romance book, it's best to leave people like Stephen King's fans alone.

When I publish my upcoming erotic romance series, I am going to find where E.L. James' audience hangs out and place ads on the sites and in the groups they frequent. But I will *never* approach any of them in reader groups, promoting my books. I will just place ads in places they will likely see them (such as Goodreads, Facebook, Amazon and BookBub). It is important not to spam and harass potential customers.

When you start marketing, here is what does not work. It didn't work for me, and I have never seen it work for anyone. Yet I see people doing it all the time. The goal here is to save you time.

WHAT DOESN'T WORK:

Posting a description of your book or the link to buy it on book promoting pages on social media does not work. I was told to do that by random authors I didn't know who were not successful. So I did it. I posted my book link and description hundreds of times for about a month on dozens and dozens of promo pages. I did not see one bit of sales increase. It was a complete waste of time. I also felt desperate when doing it.

Emailing tons of people you don't know and spamming them about your book doesn't work, so I am told. I didn't think that would work when I was told to do it. So I didn't. I have since talked to several authors who have tried it. They all said it didn't work a bit better than promoting on free social media promo pages. And last but not least …

PAYING SOMEONE to promote your book DOES NOT work. I have never done this. And I never will. I talked to numerous agencies that are operating legally about promotions. They all wanted insane prices per month to promote. While doing my research, I talked to dozens of authors who had used them. Not one single author made back in book sales what they paid the company. And not one author recommended using them. I dropped this idea. Your money is best spent buying advertisements on reputable sites like BookBub, Amazon, and Facebook, to name a few. But know what you are doing before you start spending money on the ads.

I have talked with several successful authors who said they have appeared on TV shows and podcasts, had articles done about their books, and been on several YouTube channels. All have said they did not receive any significant increase in sales afterward.

However, they still do it to talk about being an author and to help and share information with others who are just starting out, or to meet fans who have already bought their books. But it doesn't work as a promotional tool. All have said to *never* pay to be on one or pay to be in a publication.

If you are paying to be on a podcast, that is because the podcast has very few, if any, listeners. If you have to pay to be in a magazine, it is because nobody buys or reads the magazine.

It's a waste of money. Remember, the goal is to get your book in front of potential customers. You can't do that paying to be on a podcast with no listeners, on a show that nobody watches, or in a magazine that nobody reads. One of the most common scams is people who own the magazine, show, or podcast saying the fee is just to pay for the publication of it. If you have to pay to be on or in anything, it's a con. It won't help you. You may be on or in it, but what good will it do if nobody is going to see it? You are wasting money.

WHAT CAN WORK (all free stuff):

I recently left almost all of the author-related groups that I was involved with. The few that I am still a part of do not allow random book promotions. They do not allow solicitation of any services. They are genuine authors networking to help each other.

Instead of author groups, get involved with reader groups in your genre. (*Do not* promote your books here.) Just get involved in the conversations and interact with the readers. Take an interest in these people and their lives. I did this and started having a blast.

You can really find out a lot if you are in a reader group of your genre. You find out what they like and don't like to read. When you are involved in the group, the members eventually will see your profile and see you are an author. Many will check out your books without you even mentioning that you are an author.

I saw an increase in sales when I started interacting with people on social media. I did this before taking any classes or being trained in any way. Almost every class I sat through advised authors to be active on social media to increase sales. I know this works, to a degree. And I have had a lot of fun doing it. I have met some awesome people. I too have bought dozens of books that I thought I would like because I had conversations with these authors and liked their style. Not a single one of them mentioned that they were an author nor did they mention their books to me. I found out because I checked out their profile. And, by the way, the stories were some of the best I have ever read.

An absolute master at this is author Alessandra Torre. If you want to know the best way to do this, check out some of her free webinars. They last about an hour and are full of great information on social networking with readers. In fact, when you take one of her webinars, be sure to take screen shots of the notes during the class. You won't have time to write down everything she says. It is all wonderful info to have. She has an excellent class on using Goodreads to your advantage. Search for her free classes and take a few.

ADS:

Here are a few links you can use to set up ads for your books that I have been told work to a degree. I have never used any of these. I have no firsthand knowledge of how they work. But they were recommended by many of the successful, full-time, self-published, six-figure-a-year authors in several of the classes I took. I plan to use these when I advertise my new series.

FREE ADVERTISING LINKS:

https://nicholaserik.com/promo-sites/

https://kindlepreneur.com/list-sites-promote-free-amazon-books/

https://blog.reedsy.com/book-promotion-services/

HOW TO RUN ANY ADS, FREE OR PAID:

I have been advised again and again that the best way to get sales is to run one or two ads a day using different free sites. Do this three or four times a week. Example: Run a few ads on Monday, a few on Wednesday, and a few on Friday. Run the ads in different places each day you use them. When you have used every resource on the ad lists above, start over. Run the free stuff on this kind of timetable. For paid ads, once every few to six months seems to work better.

USEFUL INFORMATION:

Many vendor sites respond best when your book has a steady stream of sales. The goal is for your book to sell well all along. Most vendor sites do not like a high number of sales all at once and then a deep decline. (That's what I had.) Amazon algorithms hate this. If you can find a steady stream of customers in your genre, Amazon's algorithm eventually will start recommending your book to customers who buy books similar to yours. When this happens, your book sales will start rising. It's free advertising. Eventually, you'll get more sales for doing exactly the same thing. These vendor sites make money when you do. They want you to do well.

PAID ADVERTISING:

The most successful indie authors I have talked to have used paid ad services from some or all of the following: Facebook, Google, Goodreads, and Amazon. I have no firsthand knowledge of how to do any of these. There are tons of videos showing you how to use ads like this on YouTube if you are interested.

Hands down, the best paid ad site is BookBub.com. Every author I talked to who uses BookBub ads made back all of the money that they spent on the ad through new sales. Many make back their money within twenty-four hours. The highest return on investment that I know of an author making for a BookBub ad is $14,000 in book sales in less than a month from a featured ad that cost the author $500. Giving $500 and getting $14,000 is a great deal. Of course, not every ad will get these results. But I haven't talked to anyone yet who didn't make money by placing ads on BookBub. I have read a ton on this site and how to use ads on it. I won't go into how it works, but author David Gaughran has one of the best videos explaining it on YouTube. He uses these ads religiously, and his video is almost an hour long and well worth it. Check out David's video to get a great idea as to how this works.

Every successful indie author who has taught a class I have attended has been very clear that authors need to be social on at least one social media site and have an author website. The primary reason for a website is for fans of your work to connect with you and to entice potential readers into buying your books. Many authors do different things to accomplish this. Some run giveaways, some offer signed paperback copies, some offer bookmarks, etc. You'll have to talk to authors who have done these things. I personally have no experience with them.

An email list is a must. When someone buys your book, they are a customer. When they read your book, love it, and buy another one and love it, they will start to buy all of your books in that genre. When they get used to your writing and the feeling they get from reading your work, you have made what Sarra Cannon refers to as a loyal fan. That is the goal. If you can turn a reader into a loyal fan, they will buy everything you publish. You will then have built-in sales for each new release.

Imagine having ten thousand loyal fans and releasing three or four books a year. If you make $4 on average per book you sell, and have ten thousand loyal fans, that's more than $100,000 a year. Also keep in mind that with constant advertising, you will be bringing in new customers all along and adding to your loyal fan base.

When you are about to release a new book, you can let your loyal fans know by sending out an email. Be sure to include a link to buy your book in that email. (I was told that I wouldn't think that would need to be said. But I was also told that I'd be surprised at the authors who didn't include the link.) An author website is a great place for all fans to sign up for your mailing list.

I have not yet made my author website. I did include my email address in both my ebook and paperback. I also have been very active on social media. I have had more than 200 people ask me to email them when I have something new coming out. I have been storing all of those email addresses and will include them when I make my list. (For the record, more than 200 email addresses is a lot for someone who doesn't have an author website.)

AS FOR EMAIL LISTS:

By law, you must have a way for a person to unsubscribe on each email you send out. And if they unsubscribe, you must take them off the list. By law, each email must contain a physical company mailing address. This can be where you live, but I advise against that. Most authors get around this by using a post office box. I do know there is a cheaper way to get a physical address by going through FedEx. I don't have a clue how to do that, but I know successful authors who do it. I, personally, am going with the P.O. box.

MARKETING STRATEGY:

Now I will cover marketing strategy. So let's start with everything I have shared so far that is related to marketing, plus a few new tips:

1. Fiction books sell far better than nonfiction books.
2. A series will sell far better than a stand-alone novel.
3. Authors make more money if they stick to one genre.
4. The top selling genres are romance, psychological thriller, and sci-fi.
5. Women buy three times more books than men do.
6. Almost 70% of all books purchased are by women between ages 18 and 49.
7. If properly marketed, your book can make passive income for decades.
8. Placing a few ads every few days works better than a lot of ads placed in one day.

To give you an overall example, I am going to give you my personal marketing and business strategy for the next twelve-book series I am writing.

My business model:

I am setting up my own publishing company as an LLC. (Don't worry. I am not soliciting anyone or anyone's books, ever. The only client I am ever going to have is me. It is solely for my benefit. I will not take on anyone else.) I am setting up a publishing company where the only employees ever will be my wife and me. I have set up a bank account for that company. All of my books will be a product of my publishing company.

Each year, I will take the total profits of that company and pay my wife and me a salary while leaving enough money in the account for business expenses. (I'll cover this stuff in the business model later.)

I am going to publish all of my books through my company, including buying my first book from myself. (Yep, you can do that.) NOTE: This part is not necessary. You don't have to do it. If I weren't married, I wouldn't do it. But because my wife could be affected by my decisions, I am going this route only for liability reasons … just in case.

Why am I doing this?

Liability and tax purposes. When you talk about making more than $100,000 a year, that's a lot in taxes. I have crunched the numbers and found this would work best for me.

Also, if I am ever sued, my publishing company is an entity in and of itself. That means if someone gets pissed off and decides to sue me, my publishing company is all that can be sued. If they win, they can get only the company assets and not my personal assets. My home and personal bank account can't be touched the way I am setting things up. Also, as icing on the cake, it will look like I am published by a traditional publisher on each vendor site. But to be honest, I don't give a curly hair on a rat's behind about looking traditionally published. Most readers don't actually look at that anyway. All I care about is taxes and protection from losing assets.

My writing strategy:

I am writing all twelve books in one of the bestselling genres, romance. I am writing that romance book in the most popular selling subgenre, erotic romance. I am using the most bought tropes in romance, which are contemporary, friends-to-lovers, and small-town. In doing this, women will be my target audience.

Why am I doing this?

It will be the easiest to market. If I write in the bestselling genre, subgenre, and tropes to the audience that buys the most books, it will be a lot easier to get my book in front of the eyes of the customers who will be most likely to buy it. That is simply because there are more eyes. I am also writing to the widest gender and age range market.

Note: You should always write what you love. I AM writing what I love. But if what you love doesn't fall into this category, it will show. So write what you love and market to your target audience, even if it takes longer to be successful.

I am going to write all twelve books before I do anything. Each book will be completely finished, edited, cover designed, and formatted before I do anything else. Each cover will be branded to show that each book is related.

My publishing strategy:

When I am done writing, I am going to upload Book 1 for purchase on each vendor site while uploading Book 2 for pre-order. I am going to include a link at the end of each ebook to purchase the next book in the series that is on preorder. (Each ebook will be vendor specific. If you buy the book on Amazon, the link to purchase the next book will be an Amazon link. If you buy the book on Barnes & Noble, the link to purchase the next book will be a Barnes & Noble link.) When Book 2 is almost ready to be released, I'll put up Book 3 for pre-order and do the same thing.

I am releasing each book three months apart, for a total of four releases every year for three years. All research has shown this to be the most profitable release strategy when you are not rapidly releasing books.

During the first three months of the release of my first book in the twelve-book series, I am not doing any advertising. Instead, I am going to set up my author page, work on my email list, work on my social media presence, and have everything I need in place for the second book when it is released.

Why am I doing this?

All research has shown that a new author doesn't sell as many books as a veteran author sells. So why waste money on advertising at this point? I'll start advertising after Book 3 is released. By then I should have everything in play that I need to start really focusing on selling books.

My pricing strategy:

After I release Book 5 in my series, I am going to set Book 1 for free, Book 2 at a discount, and books 3, 4, and 5 at full price. I am going to start advertising everywhere that will allow me to advertise. I am going to focus on getting new readers and always refer them to Book 1 of the series. After Book 3, the follow-through is usually 75% or better. So if you can get a customer to read books 1, 2, and 3, usually they are hooked on the series and will pay after that.

When I get eight books out, I am going to set books 1 and 2 for free. Then I am going to set Book 3 at a discount, and books 4 and on will be full price. I am doing this for the rest of my life. You can't get more fair than that to a customer. Try books 1 and 2 for free. If you like it, Book 3 is at a discount. By then they will know whether or not to follow the series through to the end. If they like it, the sell-through should make tons of money.

Why do this?

Because this is the tried, tested and true method. The best in the business have used this very method and made millions. By the time Book 6 comes out, I should have enough time with everything in place that I can spend a few hours a week marketing my series while spending the rest of the time writing another new series. By the time my current series comes to a close a year and a half later, I should be ready to release a newer series, which also will be an erotic romance. And so on and on.

Then what?

Well, after I saw what stand-alone books make when marketed compared to what series books make when marketed, it made more sense to work on my series and push it than to market my stand-alone that I published in 2020. After my new series is published, I am going back to market the stand-alone too. My hope is that it will start selling if what I am writing now is a hit, even if it is in a different genre. My plan is to write erotic romance novels from here on out. But I hope my 2020 literary fiction novel will sell if my strategy works for my new genre.

That is my business and marketing plan. Anyone is capable of doing this without using a publisher or agent ... ever! I can do my whole twelve-book series myself without a publisher and agent. It is possible to do all of this for free.

CHAPTER 10
The Business Side Of Books

Most of this information applies to U.S. residents only. If you are in another country, you will have to check what is required for you.

BUSINESS MODELS:

As I have said, if you are publishing books on your own, you are a business. So you might want to look into different business plans. Then again, you may not want to. None of this is a must.

Many very successful indie authors just publish books and list themselves as publishers and count that as part of their income. And that is fine. There is virtually no risk considering that few authors get sued. However, there is a very small risk involved, no matter how tiny. So I'll go through the most common business structures that authors use. Research each to see what you prefer.

1) **A sole proprietorship:** This is hands down the easiest and the one that most authors use. If there is a fee for setting up a sole proprietorship in your state, it will be a small fee. Check your state's requirements to set one up. (You can apply for a federal tax number if you'd rather not use your Social Security number.)

You can check your state's requirements here:

https://www.nolo.com/legal-encyclopedia/50-state-guide-establishing-sole-proprietorship.html

2. **A Limited liability company (LLC):** This is what I use personally. The main difference between this and a sole proprietorship is that an LLC protects the owner from personal liability and debt of the business, as I discussed in the last chapter. There are some simple requirements. You have to come up with a name for your business that is not already taken by someone else. You have to fill out a lot more paperwork than with a sole proprietorship, and the fees are usually significantly higher. You'll need to contact your state's Secretary of State if you decide to go this route. It is time consuming. But it isn't difficult.

3. **S corporation:** The main difference in this is taxes. I would try to explain it, but it gets very complicated. Also, I don't have a damn clue on most of it myself. So if an S corp is something you think you might be interested in, do an online search. I do know that many authors who make millions use this business model. But I know enough about this model to know it's not for me.

Note: If you want to use a pen name to keep your identity a secret, you can file for a DBA (doing business as …) I have never done that and don't know anyone who has. But you can search it and follow directions if you choose to use a pen name.

GETTING PAID IN ROYALTIES:

This is easy. Each vendor will ask you how you want to be paid. You select your preferred way. I use a direct deposit into my company's bank account. Can't get more simple than that. But there are other ways. Many vendors will send you a monthly check if you'd like. Also, each vendor may pay slightly different royalty rates.

NOTE: This is why I recommend self-publishing, as I said in an earlier chapter. If you use a publisher, con or not, almost every publisher out there will have access to all royalty and sale information and, get this: *You will not have access to this information!* You are completely in the dark about what you make and what you sell. You will have to rely on your publisher's word.

If you self-publish and do everything yourself, you have access to all of your royalty and sale information and nobody else does ... unless you approve them to have it. I can look at my vendor and see how many books I sold on any given day since I published my book. I can see what royalty amount I made on any given day. I can see when my royalties were directly deposited into my account. I can see how many books I have sold from the very beginning. There are no questions at all. I do all my spreadsheets. I also can do my own price changes whenever I want. I don't answer to one single person or entity, ever! I swear there is nothing like it.

TAXES:

Well, this is simple. At the beginning of the year, each vendor will email you a link to a printable W2 for the year. They will give you the tax documents you need to do your taxes just like an employer would do each year. How simple is that?

ALSO A FEW TAX TIPS:

If you hire anyone to do anything author related for you, <u>and you pay them</u> more than $600 in one year, you have to fill out a tax form and send it to them. I'll never do this personally because I will never pay someone $600 in a year ever. But if you do, then Google the tax documents that you have to fill out and send.

Also, almost everything you spend on your author business is tax deductible. So keep up with those receipts. Paper, ink, computer programs, apps, printers, car mileage going to author events, meals while attending conferences, etc., can be deducted. The rules change all the time on this.

Here is a website that tells you what the government's most current rules are:

https://www.irs.gov/businesses/small-businesses-self-employed/deducting-business-expenses

AND NOW:

The reason I wrote this information is to let any author know that they can publish their own books and make tons of money without ever using a publisher. Less than a year ago, I didn't know any of this stuff. The training is out there.

I know I gave a lot of information. But I barely scraped the surface. If this seems overwhelming, just take it one simple step at a time.

BABY STEPS:

1. **Write:** You can do this for free.
2. **Edit:** Not recommended to do it yourself, but you can do this for free.
3. **Format:** You can do this for free.
4. **Design a cover:** Not recommended you do your own, but you can do this for free.
5. **Upload to as many vendors as you'd like:** You can do this for free.
6. **Start collecting your royalties:** Also free.
7. **Market:** You can do this for free ... but paid ads work much better.

That is all that is required to be a self-published author. Take each step one at a time. The steps aren't hard; they are just time-consuming. If you can't figure out how to do one of those steps yourself, pay someone a reasonable fee for the task. There are thousands of freelancers who do all of this on Fiverr.com. If there is something you want done, here's a list:

- Good editing can be done for less than $500.
- Formatting can be done for less than $50.
- A good cover design can be done for less than $100.
- There are tons of free ways to advertise. But the most lucrative way is to pay for ads.

GETTING REVIEWS:

The only way I will ever receive a review is out of the blue. I don't ask for reviews. I don't trade reviews. I don't exchange reviews with other authors. I don't send out advance reader copies (ARCs) for an honest review. And I will never, ever pay for a review. Every review that I have on my book, I have gotten out of the blue and had no idea that the review was coming.

I know giving out ARCs for an honest review is not against terms of service on even the strictest of vendors, so long as the reviewer says so in the review. But I, personally, would feel strange doing it. However, buying a review is against every vendor's terms of service. It *is* cheating. Spin that however you want. But it is unethical as hell. It's sad this is a common practice among the indie author community. *Never* pay for a review. I have left a few memes and posts on social media explaining that reviews help sell books, and asked generally for people to leave reviews of books they like. But I have never asked a particular person for a review on my book. It just doesn't feel right to me. Most of my book's reviews came from being active on social media.

I also think it is unethical to review another author who writes in my genre. I'll never leave a review of an author who writes romance like I do. I also have a personal rule: I will never give another author a bad review. If I don't like a book, I just won't leave a review. That hasn't been an issue since I started reading indie authors. I either knew the author well enough that I figured I'd like what they wrote, or I love the genre of their book. I have left a five-star review for every book I have read this year.

HOW TO HANDLE A BAD REVIEW:

This is simple. How do you handle a bad review? Do not respond in any way. *Get over it.* Move on. There is no other way to handle a bad review that will promote your success. But if you are dead set on damaging your career and reputation, a perfect way to do it is responding to a troll. Mark Twain has been credited with this quote: "Never argue with a fool; onlookers may not be able to tell the difference."

If you do all of this yourself, you are done. You will enjoy all the royalties for the rest of your life. Your books can even be making money when your grandkids have grandkids. That's a cool legacy to leave your family.

CHAPTER 11
Spotting A Con Publisher
And What To Do

Here's the deal. YouTuber Djemilah Birnie said something that stuck with me when she was talking about avoiding author scams on the internet. She basically said that there are a lot of con artists who know that new authors do not understand this industry and are willing to take advantage of that. It is very true. I have seen it every day on Facebook for more than a year. I liked the way she put it, and you might remember me saying a version of that earlier in this book.

I am going to put it a lot less nicely, myself. So pay attention to this statement. If you do not take any other advice I give, please take this advice:

No legitimate publisher is going to solicit an unknown author to publish a book they have never read. *There are no exceptions to this rule.*

Also, authors *do not* pay real publishers, ever. *There are no exceptions to this rule either.*

I spent a quarter of a century putting criminals in jail. I have no problem calling these people what they are: **CROOKS** and

<u>**CON ARTISTS**</u>! There are tons of people who do legit work for authors on social media. I am about to show you how to tell the legit people from the crooks.

FIRST OF ALL:

There is not one single publisher online looking to sign an author they have never heard of to a contract for a book they have never read. I promise. There's also no real firm or company looking to market a book they haven't read from an author they have never heard of. Does that make sense? I have more than 1.5K friends on my Facebook page. I have blocked double that number (at least 3,000 people) on social media who started to solicit me for money the second I put "author" on my profile. They are *everywhere!* Your goal as an author is to *make* money, not to *pay* money.

HERE'S WHAT THEY DO:

What they promise: We will get your book in front of the eyes of millions of people.

What they are likely to do: They get lists of real email addresses of people they have no relationship with at all. Then they spam those people by emailing them the link to your book. They also post the link on free book promotion sites on the internet.

What do we all do with spam? We delete it. Within ten minutes they have contractually fulfilled their obligation to you without helping your sales at all. I don't want my book spammed to a million people who don't give a crap about it and aren't going to buy it. I want it to get in front of ten thousand people who are interested in it and **will** buy it.

What they promise: We will get your manuscript edited, formatted, and your book "out there."

What they are likely to do: They run your manuscript through a free online editor, get someone to format it, buy or compose a cheap cover, and stick it on Amazon. They spent maybe $100 on you and they have fulfilled their obligation. Yet you paid them thousands. Did I mention they also are very likely to keep the rights to your book and most of the royalties?

Not me. I spend months writing my books. They are my babies. I am keeping them. And I sure as hell ain't paying someone to take them away.

WHAT HAPPENS ONCE YOU PAY THESE CROOKS?

Nothing! I have talked to many, many authors who have given these people thousands of dollars and gotten nothing in return except the realization that they no longer have the rights to their book and they didn't make any money.

The lowest I have had an author tell me they paid these crooks was $850.

The highest I have heard of an author paying these crooks was $25,000.

The lowest amount an author has been paid after signing with these people was zero dollars.

The most an author has told me they were paid by these criminals was $250.

You don't have to be a business major to know that the return on investment here sucks.

I have **NEVER** heard of an author who signed with a publisher that they had to pay making **ANY** money at all, **EVER**.

Keep in mind if you are starving to be published, if you give these people your book first, then realize you were conned and keep trying to promote your book later, a real publisher will never, ever touch it.

You can write your own book. Then you can pay to have it professionally edited, formatted, and covered for thousands less than you will be charged by a crook claiming to want you and your book. They don't want you or your book. They don't give a damn about you or your book. They want your money. Nothing else.

You can publish your own work to five major vendors on your own, and many more. If you have never done this before and you have never seen this done, you can do it in a single day.

Writing is the hard part. You went to elementary school. You went to high school. You may even have gone to college. You have been trained to write from a very early age. You haven't been trained in anything else author-related. Everything else is way easier to learn. It took you many, many years to learn to read and write. You can learn how to get your editing, formatting, cover design, and publishing done in a week. You can learn to market your book like a professional in a week. Just buckle down and **learn** it. Day 1 will be hard. Day 5 will be easy. You don't need a publisher.

When I say these people are "con artists" or "crooks," I don't mean they will take your money and run. What I mean is they will take your money and not do anything for you that matters. They can fulfill their contractual obligations in under an hour.

Everything they do, you could either do yourself or pay someone to do for you at a fraction of what they will charge you. A real publisher will pay you. You will **NEVER** pay a real publisher.

HOW TO SPOT A CON ARTIST:

The number one giveaway is if **they solicit you in any way.** The most popular way is social media. Take the time to stop here and look at my Facebook profile. Seriously. Take note that my real picture is on my profile page. My face is in almost all of my photos. I have multiple pictures of me with family and friends. I created my public Facebook page less than two years ago. There are plenty of posts on my main page. I have numerous interactions with people I know and who know me. I have pictures with other people that I am friends with on Facebook. Check out the people I interact with. See their profiles? There are pictures on there of me with them. I have many "likes" on my posts. All of these are indicators that my profile is genuine.

I have many friends on Facebook that have the exact same thing on their profiles. They do book covers. They do formatting. They edit and beta read. They are up front about what they offer and they aren't hiding anything. They have contact info on their page and examples of their work. There are no contracts to sign. Once they do the job you hired them to do, the relationship ends.

In contrast, almost (but not every) profile of a con publisher or marketer will have few or no pictures. They won't have interactions or "likes." Look at when they created their profile; they usually won't have had one for very long. A legit person's profile will look like mine. If they are offering a service for an author and they are legit, they will have a location and a way to contact them. They will have many examples of their work.

BEWARE: Just as many crooks have very professional-looking websites that wait for you to come to them. **Do not fall for it!** If they start talking about "author packages" and start asking for money or fees of any kind, walk away. **They are conning you.**

HOW TO TELL WHAT YOU WILL GET:

If you are approached by (or searching websites of) publishers, do this when you make contact or are contacted by someone:

Ask them: Who is your most famous author? Look up that author. Look up that author's work. You can find out who this author's publisher is on Amazon or any website where that author's book is sold. (If they give you the name of a famous author, that author may not have anything to do with them. A simple search can verify it in under a minute.) Remember, these people lie for a living.

Ask them: What are some of the books you have published and who are the authors of those books? Get the names of the books and authors and do a search on Amazon. Look at that author's rank. Are you really willing to pay for that rank? Look at that book's number of reviews and ratings. Are you really willing to pay for that number of ratings and reviews?

I spent a day looking at things like this. These crooks will post in author groups that they are "now accepting manuscripts." So I would search the publishing company and their books and authors. I was never impressed. I did better own my own, drunk, than any of these con publishers' authors did.

If all else fails, contact the author yourself and ask how their experience was with this "publisher." You will be surprised at the number of famous authors who will respond to your emails or messages. I was. The more popular they are, the longer it will take in many cases. Some will never respond to you.

A few months back I posted a comment that was very similar to the above advice.

A girl from Alabama had sent me a friend request that I had accepted without question. When I posted that no one needed a publisher and they could do everything themselves, this girl got pissed and started responding with very rude comments. A con publisher got mad at me for posting that con publishers were not needed. There's that pattern again.

She let me know that she was an author herself and that she ran a small, legit publishing company to *help* authors. She let me know that is how she made a living. So I looked at her "publishing company."

She did have a webpage where you could buy all of her books and the other authors' books (but most of the books were hers). She had a list of things that she did for authors along with the prices that she charged. Her prices were outrageously high. Each price was hundreds of dollars more than the average price you could get for the exact same service on Fiverr.com. Any author who knew the business and how things worked could tell you that she was taking advantage of new authors who didn't know any better. She wasn't *helping* new authors. She was *helping herself* to the new authors' money.

As for her signed authors? Well …

I did a search for her authors' books. Her publishing company had sixteen books on Amazon. Some of those books had been there for five years. My book had been out for not quite a year at the time. I had more reviews on my one book than she had on all of her sixteen books combined. I also had more ratings on my one book than she had on all of her sixteen books combined. And remember that the majority of those books were hers. She was the author. She wasn't even capable of promoting herself. So if you go with her "publishing" company, that is what you will be paying for.

I, on the other hand, spent $75 on my book. After I wrote my book, I did everything else myself except the formatting. It took a week of researching and following directions to have it published and ready for people to buy. If I had signed with her publishing company, I would have paid thousands of dollars for the exact same thing, and her company would have taken half my royalties for the rest of my book's life. I literally would have paid someone to take my book and my money away from me. **That ain't happening.** The thing is, she was telling authors right up front that she was conning them. Everything she charged was posted in plain view. Several new authors just didn't know any better and fell for it.

After all this, if you are still considering going with one of these small publishers, at least do this: Go to Amazon and enter that publishing company's name in the Books or Kindle department. Look at the rankings of these books. Look at the number of reviews and ratings that book has. How long has it been out? Do you really want to pay for yourself and your book to be as anonymous as that?

A few days ago I saw where an author posted in an author group on Facebook that it was impossible to make money without a real publisher. She said that she was just being honest with people and even implied they should give up writing if they couldn't get a publisher. She actually said to name one successful author who was not published by a real traditional publisher.

Let me answer her question here. Sarra Cannon, Hugh Howey, Jenna Moreci, Nick Russell, and Alessandra Torre, just to name a few off the top of my head. All are self-publishers. All are making a good living at it full time. All are in complete and total control of their work. None needed an agent or a publisher. These are just five names out of almost six thousand. All are making more money than almost 90% of traditionally published authors.

And now for the super sad truth that nobody seems to want to say. I think everyone avoids this. But it **really does** need to be said.

I am convinced that many authors want so much to brag about being a traditionally published author that they are willing to pay these high prices. Many are willing to fool themselves and the people closest to them. They are genuinely afraid to fail. I think many authors pay these people knowing full well that they aren't really traditionally published. If any of these authors are reading this, please listen to me. I got drunk and stumbled ass backwards into a #1 bestseller by accident! You *can* do this on your own. *You can! Thousands* of others *have* done it.

The truth is there are more authors making a living at self-publishing than there are authors who make a living as traditionally published authors. Yes, you read that correctly. I'll say it again. There are more authors making a living at self-publishing than there are authors who make a living as traditionally published authors. As I said earlier, people like Stephen King, J.K. Rowling, E.L. James and John Grisham are the exceptions as traditionally published authors. They are far from the rule. The overwhelming majority of traditionally published authors still have day jobs. They can't make enough money to support themselves on their royalties alone. Truth.

However, there are way more self-published authors than traditionally published authors who fail every year. And why? I think it is because once they write their book, they have no idea what to do with it. They don't take the time to research and learn the business themselves. They ask a question like "What now?" in an author group, and con artists and crooks come out to feed. Once you write your book, research the right way to publish and market. There's tons of great advice out there. Train yourself to do it. Most of those unsuccessful self-published authors failed because they did not take the time to learn the business. They never actually tried to make it.

SO WHAT DO YOU DO IF YOU'VE ALREADY BEEN TAKEN?

Let's say, just for the sake of argument, that you've read all this and now realize you signed with one of the crooks and you got screwed. What do you do?

Well, for starters, don't give the bastards another dime. **EVER!** Make damn sure that company does NOT have permission to take anything else from whatever account you used to pay them. Stop them from taking money out of your bank account, or charging your credit or debit card or PayPal account.

Then contact the crooks and explain to them that you realize they are not what they represented themselves to be and you **are** leaving the contract.

Did you know that to do business anywhere in the United States, you have to have a business license? Ask the crook where they got their business license and ask them what their permit number is to do business. (I'd be willing to bet in many cases they don't even have a license.) If they do, get the number as well as the place it was issued. Tell the crook you are filing a complaint with the agency where they have the license. If they won't tell you their permit number, you can find out for yourself. Contact the city hall of their city, or the county courthouse if they're in a county. Most people file complaints with the Better Business Bureau.

Did you know that you can file the same complaint with their state's Attorney General's office as you can file with the BBB? If you suspect they are crooks, call the IRS. Let Uncle Sam know you are concerned that they may not be filing their tax returns correctly. Al Capone killed thirty-nine people and never did a minute of jail time for it. He did die in prison for tax evasion.

You also can turn to social media and post the story of your dealings with them. It's not libel if the story is true. Be sure to take screenshots and have all the proof you need just in case they try to sue you. Remember, you have to tell the truth about what happened.

NOTE: If you signed a contract with a legit publisher and just aren't getting the results you wanted, this *does not* apply.

I personally would tell the company that I had all of the above plans ... or they could just let me out of my contract. If you dedicate your life to costing them money and grief, they might let you out of your contract to have you gone. Remember, they probably solicit new authors online. Go to all the author groups and give every author a heads up every week about the company.

Every time I post anything like what I've stated above, one of those people starts to argue with me and wants to wage an all-out war over what I have said. The reason for that is if even one person listens to me and doesn't pay them, they could lose $10,000 (this is what several of the crooks charge). If you listen to me, you and I lose nothing, but they lose money. When someone like this engages me, I delete their comments, block them, move on, and forget all about them.

CHAPTER 12
In Conclusion …

All of this information I have been giving you can be found on the internet for free. I wrote this book so you can have all the information in one place without spending months searching for it. Now I'll leave you with some of the best sites to visit for your own training.

WHERE TO GET PAID TRAINING:

- https://heartbreathings.teachable.com/p/publish-and-thrive

(This is the BEST one I attended. Hands down.)

- https://www.skillshare.com/browse/creative-writing?enrollmentType=premium&seeAll=1

(Skillshare.com has both paid and free classes for authors and writers.)

WHERE TO GET FREE TRAINING:

- https://www.inkerscon.com/free-classes
- https://www.youtube.com/c/HeartBreathings

- https://www.youtube.com/c/DavidGaughran
- https://www.youtube.com/c/JennaMoreci
- https://www.youtube.com/c/Reedsy
- https://www.youtube.com/c/Alessandratorre00

The following link has good, free training. But they will try to talk you into using only Amazon KDP in many lessons. Don't fall for it if it doesn't fit your needs.

- https://www.youtube.com/c/Kindlepreneur

RECOMMENDED BOOK FOR MORE ON THE SUBJECT OF SELF-PUBLISHING:

- https://www.amazon.com/Write-Publish-Repeat-No-Luck-Required-Self-Publishing/dp/1629550523/

That brings me to the end of my information. I do hope that this gives you enough information so you can see that you can do everything on your own. But the reason I wrote all this stuff down is so new and aspiring authors can clearly see: You *do not* need a publisher or an agent to be successful as an author.

The days where you had to have a publisher to make money writing books died more than a decade ago. Print on demand killed that need. In fact, I have been doing this for a year and a half. I have seen that need decrease considerably during just that time.

I'm basically giving away this information. The information belongs to everyone. However, my words are copyrighted. Don't think I won't have my lawyer sue the hell out of someone who tries to copy this writing and make money from it. This particular writing belongs to me.

I am giving away all of this information in this writing to anyone who wants to use it. If you have it, give it to any author you think can benefit from it. Post it anywhere you want. Share it with everyone. I don't mind. Get this information out there. You can use in any way you want except to make a profit.

JUST REMEMBER THE RULES TO LIVE BY AS AN AUTHOR:

1) **A real publisher DOES NOT solicit authors.** A real publisher is never going to solicit you in any way by social media, message, phone, text message, at a convention, or anywhere else. If you are being solicited by someone calling themselves a publisher, run. It is a scam. There are no exceptions to this rule.

2. **A real agent DOES NOT solicit authors.** A real agent is never going to solicit you in any way by social media, message, phone, text message, at a convention, or anywhere else. If you are being solicited by someone calling themselves an agent, run. It is a scam. There are no exceptions to this rule.

3. **A real publisher will never charge an author for anything, ever.** The great authors did not make money by paying their publisher. They made money by getting paid by their publisher. Stephen King does not pay his publisher. Stephen King's publisher pays him. The publisher makes money from the author through book sales in the form of royalties. If anyone claiming to be a publisher asks you for money or a fee, run. It is a scam. There are no exceptions to this rule.

4. **A real agent will never charge an author for anything, ever.** The great authors did not make money by paying their agents.

A real agent gets paid by taking a percentage of royalties. The industry standard is 15%. Stephen King does not pay his agent. Stephen King's agent gets paid by getting a percentage of his royalties. The agent makes money when the book sells. If anyone claiming to be an agent asks you for money or a fee, run. It is a scam. There are no exceptions to this rule.

5. **A real marketing firm or marketer DOES NOT solicit authors.** A real marketing firm or marketer is never going to solicit you in any way by social media, message, phone, text message, at a convention, or anywhere else. If you are being solicited by someone calling themselves a marketer, run. It is a scam. There are no exceptions to this rule.

6. **No person and/or entity can promise you a TV deal, a movie deal, a #1 best seller, or anything else. NOTHING legit can be guaranteed. Ever.** Run from anyone who tries to tell you they can hand you all of the hopes and dreams that every author has … for a fee. There are no exceptions to this rule.

KNOW THESE RULES. FOLLOW THESE RULES. DON'T GET CONNED.

If you would like some great examples of self-published authors and their works, here are just a few of my favorites. Many of these authors have already applied these techniques and are making bank. Some are just getting started and will soon be making bank. All of them are awesome.

- https://hughhowey.com
- https://www.alessandratorre.com/all-books
- https://sarracannon.com
- https://www.jennamoreci.com

- https://www.hmbrandon.com
- https://www.leighmhall.com
- https://www.gypsyjournalrv.com (this is NYT bestselling author Nick Russell's blog)
- https://www.fallonraynes.com/books
- http://jerryhack.com
- https://www.sofiaaves.com
- https://djemilah.com

SOURCES FOR CHECKING IF A PUBLISHER IS A CON ARTIST:

- https://www.sfwa.org/other-resources/for-authors/writer-beware/
- https://www.facebook.com/WriterBeware

NOTE: Just because a publisher isn't on this list **DOES NOT** mean they are not a crook. It could mean they just haven't been complained on yet.

WRAPPING IT UP:

I am going to put a cheap version of this book for sale online for those who don't catch it going around on social media. The only reason I am putting it up for sale is that the major vendors will not let me distribute it for free. I am selling this work for the lowest price I can set.

If you're interested in the book I wrote, drunk, and accidentally got a #1 bestseller flag by it,

here's the link:

https://www.amazon.com/Retirement-TW-Robinson/dp/B08DSNCSSD/

Look me up on FaceBook and message me if you have any questions.

Or email me at: authortwrobinson@gmail.com. I'll be glad to help any way I can.

Happy writing, and love you all!

Your fellow author,

TW Robinson

Copyright © 2022.

Printed in Great Britain
by Amazon

80141454R00068